To Hortensia —

It's a beautiful place that
Henry and I find ourselves.
To share it with you
makes it perfect.

Warmest Regards

Don West
San Antonio, Texas
May 1985

THE TEXAS HILL COUNTRY

INTERPRETATIONS BY THIRTEEN ARTISTS

Number Five: The Joe and Betty Moore Texas Art Series

THE TEXAS HILL COUNTRY

INTERPRETATIONS BY THIRTEEN ARTISTS

Paintings by

KELLY FEARING • MICHAEL FRARY • JOHN GUERIN • WOODY GWYN • WILLIAM HOEY

WILLIAM LESTER • IVAN McDOUGAL • CLAY McGAUGHY • ANCEL E. NUNN

E. M. "BUCK" SCHIWETZ • EMILY GUTHRIE SMITH • E. GORDON WEST • RALPH WHITE

Introduction by A. C. GREENE   *Foreword by* JOHN PALMER LEEPER

TEXAS A&M UNIVERSITY PRESS
College Station

Library of Congress Cataloging in Publication Data
Main entry under title:

The Texas hill country.

   (The Joe and Betty Moore Texas art series ; no. 5)
   1. Painting, American—Texas—Catalogs. 2. Painting
Modern—20th century—Texas—Catalogs. 3. Texas hill
Country (Tex.) in art—Catalogs. I. Greene, A. C.,
1923-   . II. Fearing, Kelly. III. Series: Joe and
Betty Moore Texas art series ; no. 5.
ND230.T4T5   759.164   81-40400
ISBN 0-89096-116-6   AACR2

Manufactured in the United States of America

First edition

Contents

Foreword

Whether one is on the Gulf Coast or on the flat, endless plains or in the rolling Hill Country, one is always aware of the vast spaces of Texas. The enormous sky usually is an unrelieved, intense blue, the sun is relentless, the atmosphere crystalline and unshadowed, so that even faded colors remain distinct and clean. Everything is spacious and open.

But most Texans, especially West Texas ranching and country people, speak in low voices. They may be trenchant, but rarely are they loquacious—they are accustomed to silence; the unspoken is telling; decisions are made in private. They like to be alone.

Correspondingly, the artist/poet is apt to seek, and find, silence and solitude and shadows in what is ordinarily thought of as an extroverted, boisterous world. Thus, it can be no surprise that the paintings in this portfolio are virtually unpeopled. True, a group of horsemen pause on a bluff overlooking a stream in Clay McGaughy's *Stopping Place*. True, a few figures trudge up a hill in Ralph White's *A Walk in the Hills*, and there is a bare reflection of someone in Emily Guthrie Smith's *Water*, but other than that, these fields are empty, the buildings unoccupied, and there are no humans relating one to another. Nor is there the expected wildlife: an occasional bird hangs in mid-air, or an isolated deer stands motionless. Only in Kelly Fearing's work are the animals animated and of personality, and even there the intent is other than illustrative.

The casual life of the Hill Country and the dominating presence of nature inevitably attract artists. One naturally expects twelve different talents to speak in as many vernaculars, for the Hill Country is not one thing, but many. Some artists see its tawny aridity; one may find its dark, silent pools while others respond to its spacious evening skies. But it lures them, and we share in the amusement of one, the drama of another, the different poetries of each.

The vision of Buck Schiwetz is uncomplicated: he draws and paints the country he loves with ease and directness, seeing it just as it is. *The Baldwin House near Ingram*, with its crisp drawing, is an immediate, witty response to a familiar scene. He adds washes of color or touches of crayon as a decorative afterthought, but his real skill lies in the precise images he captures. He is not concerned with the metaphysical, or the darker side of nature, but relishes instead the grazing goats, or the birds assembling around water on the *Circle J Ranch near Wimberly*. He brings an innocent eye, an adroit pencil, and great good humor to the countryside.

Similarly, Emily Guthrie Smith sees the Hill Country much as an impressionist saw the sunny French countryside, enjoying it without comment. The clear colors of her expertly handled pastels lie lightly on the surface, and her blue, untroubled waters glitter as at Giverny. It is a happy scene she depicts in *Summer River*, suggesting walks and wading on a June day. Only in *Summer Heat* is there a different potency. Here, the color has been drained by the white light, and the gray barns sit isolated and silent, shimmering in the heat.

Michael Frary is forthright. He knows exactly what he is doing; his compositions are decisive, with brilliant contrasts of light and dark, and his brushwork is authoritative and virile. Mr. Frary rarely is ineffectual, and his descriptions, his visual statements about the Hill Country, are categorical. There is no place for the implied or the nuance. One senses the sweep and energy that are characteristic of the Southwest. He brought these same qualities to his celebrated sequences of paintings of the Big Thicket and the Great Plains.

By contrast, Clay McGaughy is much more pensive. There is a kind of personal modesty about his work, as though he did not want to intrude. His deer in a snowstorm lift up their ears in alarm, but he somehow assures them that he will not come too near. His *Portrait of a River* has a restraint, even a private timidity, particularly in comparison to the clarion notes of Frary's *Sun through Clouds, Lake Travis.*

Nor does Ivan McDougal disturb or rearrange the landscape he has entered. Rather, he records it affectionately, enjoying the sparkling streams, the washed rocks, the leafless groves of trees. It is a limpid, untroubled world that he paints with calm assurance. One is with a quiet camper, a hunter without a gun.

William Hoey sees the Hill Country primarily in painterly terms. The silken surfaces of his oil washes capture its spaciousness and breeziness; no details disturb his conception of its openness. Even in his fluently painted *Wildflowers* the crisply executed trees and grasses are subordinate to the big sky and vast landscape. He paints broadly, and there is a tumultuous quality in clouds, even in rocks. And again one is in an unpopulated wilderness.

Hoey's light, liquid touch contrasts sharply with the enamelled paintings of Ancel Nunn, who lovingly records the single blade of brown or white grass. Again there is the flat blue sky, almost expressionless, that appears in so many Texas paintings, but before it Nunn will place a meticulously rendered stone house, or he will interrupt it, as in *Luckenbach Store*, with the dramatic silhouette of live oak trees. The store is an abandoned structure, its weathered wood wall checkered with bright Pepsi or Coca Cola signs. Nunn has a keen sense of value and light, and gives one much to examine and ponder. These are not simply vacant buildings, for they have poignancy and suggest a plot, a rather sinister one. The use of the broken and discarded has become a cliché, and rarely is it imbued with this genuine drama.

Drama is quickened and intensified in the majestic paintings of Woody Gwyn. His great rock rising from dark, still water is much more than a familiar scene in the Hill Country. It is ominous and primeval, and there is something pending in this silent, secret place. He is not recording, but creating. Now we are in the company of the artist/poet who searched for and found resonant silence. Perhaps even more dramatic is his *Night Silver*: the great curving land mass is dark, almost black, and the body of water is a sheet of violet edged with silver. Again there is absolute silence, and we are in the presence of unnamed forces. Flying across the ocean at night, one sometimes has this rather eerie experience of seeing the endless hammered silver surfaces of water slowly broken by mysterious, unpopulated islands or coasts. It is a world without reference.

A similar privacy pervades the more abstract, amorphous canvases of John Guerin. Never an artist to record a particular moment in time or to relate an anecdote, he uses saturated blues, rich greens, and beiges to establish mood instead. He is unhurried and somber. Guerin tells us, the spectator, nothing of himself, and he remains distant, as though we were on another hilltop but listening to the same evening song.

E. Gordon West has a strong sense of composition, using his blacks effectively and dramatically, achieving and heightening the characteristic profile. His trained brush captures a sense of aridity and desolation. He can transform the ordinary into the extraordinary, giving it a strength and significance beyond the intrinsic. His watercolor *The Train Doesn't Stop Here Anymore* is an abandoned Hill Country rural station, of which there are many, and even more paintings of them. But here the structure looms menacingly, larger than life; the perspective of a broken, splintered station platform plunges directly to it. The tonality of grays, tans, and blacks increases the ominous mood; it is a setting for Durenmatt. And again, there is nothing simply illustrative or picturesque.

The accomplished William Lester, a master over most, turned his back on the ingratiating tradition of Texas landscape painting as exemplified by Robert and Julian Onderdonk and found instead the ungainly shapes of cactus, the raw colors of earth. He created a new palette and a new iconography and led generations of Texas artists to an expressionistic interpretation of their surroundings. There is a new kind of romance to be found in the rich, succulent paint surfaces, in his strong patterns and contrasts. He conjures an untamed country.

The paintings of Ralph White included in this portfolio were done primarily between 1958 and 1963, not long after he had returned to Texas and was still exploring the region and absorbing its influence. At that time he, too, dealt with the tumultous rather than the lyrical. In *Lake in the Hills* a twisted, tortured trunk before a glowering sky becomes a swirling composition. *A Walk in the Hills* reveals his concern with textures and broad surfaces, while the people taking that walk are incidental. From the beginning, White's conception was cosmic, not illustrative.

Kelly Fearing strikes a different chord in scale and in vision. Here is a miniature, secret world populated in one instance with little armadillos moving in an almost lunar landscape among ancient, glistening boulders. Even his *Coon Fishing* is far removed from a painting of an engaging animal: the coon is not really on land or in water, and neither are the exotic fish he seeks. Armed with his meticulous sensitivity to texture and surface, Fearing had created a world beyond reality, one intimate rather than cosmic, and he has quixotically populated it with beguiling denizens of the Hill Country who probably never will be thought of again in their customary surroundings.

None of these artists departs too far from an immediate reference to a land he cherishes. His response to it may be rapturous, simply descriptive, or analytical, but the land itself remains his well-spring. This is in the strongest American tradition, and perhaps no other painter, century after century, remains so much in awe, so much in love with his native land, as does the American.

John Palmer Leeper

May, 1981

9

The Hill Country

The Hill Country, to those beauty-denied parts of Texas that lie below it, is a sudden revelation. Within just a few miles of their coastal plains and blackland prairies, it has granite mountains, rocky gorges, and softly wooded hills. It has white-water rivers, rippling streams, and gushing springs, all clear and cold. Its elevation provides cool summer nights without the buzzing insects that plague lowland visitors back home. Unlike wide stretches of the state of Texas, it has a full cycle of seasons. In the fall, against a background of yellow, gold, and red leaves, it offers the hunter a bountiful harvest of deer and wild turkey. Winter shows its face, but seldom with an ugly, icy tooth, and spring can be an astonishment of wild, natural color.

But what the Hill Country finally offers surpasses the delights of the eye and the pleasures of the flesh. It is a place of unravished quietness, where you can escape; of aloneness without isolation— a place of dreams and philosophers, and the fact that it is apt to arouse the philosopher in the most earthbound of us adds to its attraction.

I have a personal Hill Country vision: the noise of the creek below my bedroom window coming to me through the night, or, on a summer afternoon, hearing the sound of the wind through a vulture's wingtips as it drifts, unknowing, below my seat on a ledge. It is the pervasive fragrance of cedar trees and of wood smoke from my own chimney, vistas down valleys where the hand of man is present only in a rock wall or rusty barbed-wire fencing, chuck-will's-widow pleading on a spring night, owls talking from an indistinct point in the dark, a canyon wren's tumbling song.

Those are private memories, kept from a time when I was living there, outside the embrace of a city, dominated by nature but free from addresses and telephones and counting this and that, free from the tyranny of numbers—and free, if I chose, from time.

The landscape is so *right* for it all: log and limestone houses and barns, fresh water flinging itself between rocks and over falls or bubbling from the hillside to become one of those charming, unnamed rivulets which makes its way (in all but the droughtiest seasons) to some clear-bedded creek, the water sliding under limestone bluffs, hurrying to the Colorado, the Guadalupe, the Pedernales, or another of the rivers that drain this territory.

I like the idea of living amongst deer, even when they leap your deerproof fence and chew up your garden, even when an almost human bucksnort at your elbow, some dark, country night, freezes your bones for one alien instant. Arising at first light once, I opened my front door to surprise a yardful of deer. On the instant of hearing my presence, the twenty or more of them came together in a line, and with the grace of a skilled ballet company, they undulated over the fence and, continuing in file, forded the creek, wove their way uphill on the other side, and disappeared into the brush, still together in a living chain.

But deer are not always the gentle, shy creatures we believe them to be. One midnight I left my little rock office to walk up to what we called (with a touch of grandeur) the big house. The path took me through a fenced enclosure someone in the past had named "the garden." I carried a Coleman lantern, a common companion of nights in the Hill Country. As I stepped through the narrow opening in the tall wire fence, advancing toward the center of the garden, I realized the enclosure was full of deer that had become dark, shapeless missiles hurtling around me, passing so close I felt the wind and smelled the alarm. I realized the lantern was blinding them and that I was in great danger, for there must have been a dozen deer trapped in there with me. I huddled over the lantern, not daring to cut off the light but trying to give the panic-stricken deer a chance to escape the pen. I tell you, those were minutes like eternities, the blinded animals bolting through the night, filling the space with flung bodies and flying hooves—a hit by either guaranteeing a serious, or mortal, wound. Yes, indeed, deer can kill people. Ask a Hill Country native.

Obviously I escaped. One by one the deer found instinct enough to sail over the fence (fixed at the supposedly "deer-proof" eight-foot height), some of them first hitting the wire like tennis balls fired into the net and rebounding some distance to roll agilely to their feet and try again. It was a beautiful sight, even in the turmoil and danger. Eventually there were only two frightened deer and one scared man. One deer balled into the fence an incredible number of times before soaring gracefully over a low corner. But the last one failed to clear the top, hanging there by his front legs. Now I faced a dilemma: the buck on the wire was thrashing and flailing his hind legs so that it was suicidal to approach within six feet, yet if he was not detached, somehow, he would kill himself in panic. Just as I decided to muffle my face with the heavy coat I was wearing and go to his rescue, the deer somehow jerked free and climbed and tumbled to freedom—his and mine.

Drawing boundaries on an idea is dangerous, and the Hill Country is idea as much as place. Geologists talk of the Edwards Plateau, the Llano Uplift, the Balcones fault zone, all part of its definition, but only a part, the physical part. Certainly the Edwards Plateau creates much of the Hill Country's character. That vast tableland stretches southward from San Angelo and ends abruptly at the Balcones fault line, marked by the hills and cliffs of the Balcones Escarpment. With a little imagination we can see the Hill Country as the toe of the Edwardian boot thrust deep into Texas. It is only a narrow, ragged edge of the boot, but it is most deeply influenced and almost wholly marked by the geology and nature of the Edwards Plateau. The soil, for example, is very thin, and only along the rivers and in the watered valleys will you find trees much above scrub size. Yet one of the anomalies of the Edwards Plateau is that despite creating the biggest springs and some of the major rivers of Texas, it is essentially waterless. This means it is cattle, sheep, and goat country, only infrequently furnishing enough arable land to raise some vegetable and grain crops. Pecan trees grow well (and wild) along some of the waterways, and knobby-kneed cypresses, looking strangely out of place so far from the East Texas swamps, are found along perennially flowing streams like the Guadalupe River. Peaches flourish in sections of the Hill Country—Stonewall is famous for its peaches and its peach brandy—and successful experiments with wine grapes have taken place along the Guadalupe and around Fredericksburg. But even the best Hill Country farms are small and have to be carefully tended to produce a surplus.

Austin and San Antonio sit at the edge of the Hill Country, parts of both cities actually climbing the Balcones Escarpment, but neither counts as a true Hill Country community. Remember, the physical definitions are imprecise and, at best, of secondary importance when it comes to establishing the whys of Hill Country attraction. The geography of the Hill Country can be generally expressed as a crescent, or half-moon, formed by the Balcones Escarpment from San Antonio to Austin. The line then goes up the Colorado River to Llano, curving southward (generously), by way of Fredericksburg, Kerrville, Bandera, and Boerne, back to the fault line. This arbitrary boundary stops the Hill Country short of some higher hills, some beautiful springs and rivers, and several picturesque canyons lying a step or two away, but, as said, the Hill

Country is an idea as much as a place.

As a place, then, it is a place of small towns, a place of roads instead of highways, a place blessed, to an outsider's eye, by the absence of petroleum production. There are a few larger towns: San Marcos, a tourist center as well as home of Southwest Texas State University, situated on the slope of the Balcones Escarpment and a major gateway to the heart of the Hill Country; New Braunfels, another gateway, enhanced by its old German background; Kerrville, dude ranch and camp center, home of Schreiner College as well as the Schreiner family enterprises. There are other fair-sized towns like Llano, Marble Falls, Fredericksburg, Johnson City, Blanco, Wimberly, Comfort, Ingram, but the little communities are what give the Hill Country an extra dimension beyond natural beauty, because the little communities are still *there* acting like human centers, not just crossroads. There are charming places with charming names like Smithson Valley, Sisterdale, Fischer's Store, Dripping Springs, Bee Caves, Hye, Kendalia—communities remaining quaint but useful and, to date, not too disturbed by urban encroachment. The outside took a long time getting into the Hill Country, and some of the attempts have been historic failures. There is a lost monument of sorts in Kendall County: the 920-foot tunnel of the Fredericksburg & Northern Railroad, one of only two main-line rail tunnels in Texas. The road, locally built and operated, lasted less than thirty years. It just wasn't needed.

The massive front fence of the Balcones Escarpment helped to keep people and highways out, which is good, because if there is one thing the Hill Country doesn't need any more of, it's people. The thin soil can't carry humans. It has a hard enough time taking care of cattle and goats. Those clear streams can't handle human detritus much more than they are handling it now. Fortunately, except for visitors who want summer homes and retirement cottages, the Hill Country doesn't offer much incentive for increasing its population. The real tourist attractions are around the edges: Comal Spring at New Braunfels, whose two hundred million daily gallons form the Comal River, which rises and falls within the city limits; the San Marcos Springs, now highly commercialized; Barton Springs at Austin, citified into a swimming pool. The great caverns of Texas are there: Cascade at Boerne, with a ninety-foot waterfall inside; Longhorn, at Burnet; Century at Boerne, fifty million years old; Natural Bridge at New Braunfels; and Wonder World at San Marcos.

A place to get away—my favorite hideout from the wrong things. I can go there and escape from whatever is chasing me, invest in myself, and, drawing on very personal experience again, work at my profession better than at any other spot I have found in several years' searching. Once, during my residence in the Hill Country, I composed, wrote, submitted, and sold (soothing thought) three full-length books, all of which were conceived and produced between the end of April and the beginning of October. I sat in my little stone house, built years before by a family with one of those familiar Hill Country German-sounding names, and worked contentedly all day.

Before my window, my presence hidden by new screen wire, paraded armadillos, raccoons, marches of wild turkeys from strutting gobbler to six-inch chick (and they are among the shyest of Hill Country fauna), and individual deer. I even watched snakes peer cautiously from the underbrush, sliding and looping along the path the wild things took, and once a huge rattler, obviously encasing a newly swallowed varmint of some kind, heading for its nest to digest the windfall.

In the creek below our bluff I could occasionally observe raccoons washing their food ("wash bears," one former resident called them), and for days I watched a big aquatic presence pushing from shore to shore on the pond which formed just above our twenty-inch waterfall. "Nutria," an expert shrugged, but it turned out to be a Texas beaver making a comeback in the Hill Country. (There had been nutria, too, but the beaver seemed to have driven them out).

I would step from my writing cell, every now and then, to simply gaze off across the green valley and the blue hills or watch the buzzards drift and spiral—so lovely aloft and so ugly alight—and I would listen for the voices on the wind: natural voices calling or warning and the voices of the forgotten inhabitants of the place, yelling or crooning in old, undecipherable accents. And sometimes I would watch the storms shape up, moving dark and blue, becoming purple as they approached my bluff, now and then skipping my hideout altogether with their summer burden of lightning and rain, but always disturbing me with thunder and exciting me with some memory older than human recording.

Inspiration to write was, for me, universal in the Hill Country. Again, I suspect it is not just the inspiration to write; it is the inspiration to create, to make something tangible or intangible of ideas. Only one of the books on which I labored was connected in plot with the region, but the inspiration to create came in through all my senses as they were stirred by my surroundings. One learns the real meaning of *sensual* in a spot like that, away from human visibility, although not remote from human company. The Hill Country isn't the answer to urban problems—it just gives the urbanite who is seeking answers time and place to find some. Perhaps that is why so many artists and craftsmen from outside its realm have moved to the Hill Country to work.

Being a romantic of sorts, I prefer fog. Or misty rain. It fogs more than it rains in the Hill Country. If you get up early enough, down in the hollows and along the creeks you plunge into a thick, woolly blanket. Driving a car on such mornings, you have to feel for the roadway, especially if you must cross a narrow low-water bridge. And the Hill Country, as soon as you get off the main highways, clings to its low-water bridges the way Vermont clings to its covered bridges. In fact, the low-water bridge might make a more reasonable symbol for life in the Hill Country than even the lime-stone houses and barns.

There are probably a good many urbanized Texans who don't know what a low-water bridge is, although it's fairly easy to guess that it's a bridge that is subject to the rise and fall of water in its creek, branch, or river. What it amounts to is a paved bottom over which a thin stream of water is allowed to run during dry times and over which quite a flood can pour during wet times. A certain frugal realism is displayed in low-water bridges. They are simple and not costly to construct, and most of the time one may drive over them with only two to six inches of water flowing by, or even dry-tired if the low-water bridge has been built with a drainpipe running underneath the slab. They have no railings to mark their location during heavy flooding.

Long-term residents learn not to gauge flood stage on their personal creeks by the amount of rain falling in the immediate vicinity. They can tell you of times when they have watched a rise come tumbling down some stream with not a cloud in the sky overhead. Barton Creek, which West Austin considers its private, tame pleasure stream, heads many miles away in Hays County, and a heavy rain west of Dripping Springs can cause Barton to come racing toward Austin with a two-foot "ball," as it's called, under pretty sunshine. When it comes to rivers, this phenomenon can be tragic. The Pedernales, Blanco, and Guadalupe river watersheds have produced this kind of flash flooding which has cost numerous lives and millions of dollars of property damage since 1950 alone. Thus, driving onto a strange low-water bridge during floodstage can be risky, especially at night, because a mild little six-inch-deep rill can become an eight-foot-deep death trap if your car or pickup noses off, or is pushed off, the path.

One of the ardent memories from a childhood that included a few years of relatively pioneer Texas motoring involves a flooding low-water bridge in the Hill Country. Driving through toward San Antonio, my father, mother, grandmother, and I came to a flooding creek—in fact, it may have been Barton Creek where it crossed the

Llano Highway in those days. It was midnight, or near it, and the rain was still falling. Our canvas-topped, wooden-spoked Chevrolet (with leaking side curtains) joined several other vehicles to sit brooding in the wet beside the roaring water. One of the other vehicles was a big passenger bus of the period—the kind with the motor out front and a mock observation deck rear end. It was very dramatic, there in the midnight rain, headlights flickering (from both banks) on the rushing waters of the creek where it completely submerged the low-water bridge, the location of which was discernable by a leaping, bulging wave that defied even the big bus to try and breast it. I doubt if many of us were natives to the region; Hill Country folks, particularly in that day, were too smart to be out that late.

My father became a heroic figure that night, which is why I remember it all so well after half a century. He went around to all the cars, and the bus, asking who had a rope. Ropes were very nearly as common as tire pumps for Texas driving at the time, so virtually every vehicle could supply something in the way of heavy hemp. Using something an older brother had told him was done in France during the Great War, my father lined up all the cars on our side of the creek, front to rear, with the bus last in line. Then he and the others lashed front bumpers to rear, making a sort of auto train. The first car in line, with its motor off so it wouldn't drown out, was pushed onto and across the flooded bridge, then when it was safely through high water, its driver started his motor again and helped pull those behind, the vehicles, being lashed together, keeping any one of them from being washed off the bridge, as might have been the case had they tried it alone.

I have been waiting ever since to use this solution to a low-water bridge in flood. Through several years of living in the Hill Country, and being forced to cross notorious low-water bridges to reach two different homes, I waited. Not only do modern motorists not carry ropes, but you can't even find a way to lash modern automobile bumpers together. Besides, the smart alecks now have enough four-wheel-drive trucks and pickups to plunge right in and not give a low-water bridge a second thought.

All this within a landscape populated by ghosts and history. Like all remote areas, the Hill Country troubles us that once gods lived here, or some huge race that still longs to repossess the land, in those silent stretches, those cut-off valleys that are so untouched and unchanged by the feeble populations that have followed them. And in a place of stone, there can be but one appropriate symbol of history left on this land from the hand of man: flint spear points and scrapers of prehistory; ancient rock fences laid up in the almost forgotten art of dry-wall masonry; an old stone farmhouse; a rock pen; the carefully placed floor of a milk shed you discover when you scrape away a generation of debris.

Even if the sky is full of stars (and stars can be seen in lovely, low clusters in the Hill Country), the land broods. There are people here, and if their presence is invisible, the effect is not. Maybe it comes from something as simple, and as prevalent, as a local legend: Old Man Triemier and his aged only brother who killed each other at that spot, over there, in an argument about a common fence corner; the old woman who spent thirty-two years on a Travis County farm without once visiting Austin and who carried her husband's body in the buggy beside her when he died, taking it into town, dumping it (more or less) at the front door of the undertaking establishment, and announcing that the undertaker could do whatever he wanted with it, she'd pay to have it buried, but not on *her* place. When you drive by those legendary sites, even under the August sun, you tend to see things—something at the edge of the clearing where the old house stood, alongside a lonely chimney marking a spot where, for a hundred years, lives were lived with all the richness and turmoil that even the dullest life involves.

Ghosts of peoples and occupations now lost haunt the land: the charcoal burners who tended their fires, day and night, along that stretch of the Guadalupe called "Charcoal City," done in by technology, for their charcoal was not for backyard barbecuing but for uses that no longer use it and industries that no longer need it. Even the cedar choppers, that fiercely independent, untamed segment of Hill Country society that once could be found (and heard) thumping away in the cedar brakes, are disappearing, and where they survive, they no longer live up to the name, because the power saw has replaced the old cedar ax as the tool of the trade. Or you might encounter old Lyman Wight, the Mormon high priest who led his followers on a twelve-year pilgrimage through Travis, Burnet, Llano, Gillespie, Kerr, and Bandera counties, stopping at Mormon Mill, at Zodiac, and at Mountain Valley in quest of a new Zion back in the 1840s and '50s.

The felt unseen is what makes the Hill Country a special Texas place, that mysterious sort of land that never seems to let go of its memories or its past. You think you won't notice it? Try turning off the highway, late some night, onto a back road or a ranch trail. How many shapes will look like an antique beast still roaming the hills from that 1850s experiment when the U.S. Army tried to establish a camel corps at Campe Verde? And if long association with a place tends to create legends, travel around Kerrville and watch for the patriarch Charles Armand Schreiner, who began his family's still-continuing fortunes with a mercantile store (still operating) after the Civil War. He's said to persist in a nightly vigil. Or surely one can expect the presences of his sons Louis and Fritz, who lived here to the ages of ninety-nine and ninety-six, respectively. Look for tracks made in the eighteenth and nineteenth centuries which have not since been trod in by other feet: those Spanish soldiers and padres, passing through on their way to establish San Saba Mission, or possibly to work the legendary Lost San Saba Mine. Colonel Jack Hays, the magnificent Texas Ranger for whom Hays County is named, is standing off a whole tribe of Comanches (to hear him tell it) from the summit of Enchanted Rock, if you climb up on or camp near that enormous, night-singing extrusion of granite that emerges north of Fredericksburg. Then walk through the little cemeteries around Miller Creek and Cypress Creek reading the headstones which moan: KILLED BY THE INDIANS. Feel your own scalp just to be sure you're not eerily returned to join their age. And do not be afraid if, on the backroads of Loyal Valley and Cherry Springs, you meet up with Herman Lehmann, that last captive released by the Comanches, because underneath the trappings of the Indian brave there is a genial, forgiving spirit caught between two civilizations.

And everyone who enters the Hill Country must be prepared to meet the ghost of Lyndon Baines Johnson, thirty-sixth president of the United States. To the nation—to the world—he discovered and defined the Texas Hill Country. He used it as a textbook, and as a hideout, too. Drive Ranch Road 1 around his ranch, cross the long low-water bridge over (or under) his Pedernales River, taking care to pronounce it as he did and his neighbors do: Perd-*nal*-iss. And approaching the grove of huge oaks that shade the family cemetery where he is buried, you will see that tall figure standing waiting for you, or riding uneasily along on a horse (he always appeared to be slightly uncomfortable horseback), anxious to assert ownership, unable to relinquish his claim. "The best fertilizer for a piece of land," he said, "is the footprints of the owner." This was—this is—his piece of land.

And if you cannot see any of this, then turn around and go back to Houston or Dallas or some other concrete city where asphalt has exorcized both ghosts and history.

If the landscape—the rocks, bluffs, creeks, springs, deer, turkeys, cypress trees—is the natural definition of the Hill Country, then the human definition is German. The personality of the Hill Country is Germanic, just as its tongue, tortured and twisted by a century and a half of Texas, still holds the accent. Although they were never the sole proprietors, and today are long since outnumbered by the ethnic collection that surrounds them, when a Texan says Hill Country, he thinks first (and sometimes exclusively) of its

German inhabitants.

The Hill Country (which wasn't called that until the twentieth century) was nobody's land until near the middle of the nineteenth century, when it was colonized by German immigrants who came to Texas under the auspices of the Adelsverein, an association of noblemen formed in 1842 for the purpose of purchasing land in the "Free State of Texas." But by 1844 the noblemen's association had been unable to get the land originally sought, so the purpose was changed to *protection* of German immigrants. As events happened, it was the noblemen who needed protection. Their first land purchase turned out to be the frontier equivalent of buying (if I may be pardoned an anachronism) the Brooklyn Bridge. The land didn't belong to the gentleman that sold it to them. Prince Carl of Solms-Braunfels, the *verein* commissioner-general, undertook the next purchase of nearly four million acres, and it was another (almost literally) slaughter of the innocents. This tract lay far up the Colorado and Llano rivers in the heart of the Apache and Comanche range. Not even the Texas Rangers dared camp there.

But the first settlers were already landing at Carlshafen (later named Indianola) and had to be taken care of, so Prince Carl purchased enough land on the Comal River to give each family about ten acres apiece, and the city of New Braunfels (named for the prince's hometown) was begun.

Germans came pouring into Texas, and the real godfather of the Hill Country turned out to be Baron Otfried Hans Freiherr von Meusebach, who took over as commissioner-general after Prince Carl had made a less than notable success of the job. Meusebach is why the Hill Country is German. Where his predecessors had predicted happy, healthy, prosperous colonies immediately, he accepted what he found: wooded hills, rocky fields, and soil which might be six inches deep in a valley but everywhere else was more likely to go half an inch. He also found Comanche Indians who were frustrated and outraged by the Texans and were not inclined to differentiate between one kind of white man and another.

Meusebach did the practical things. First, he dropped his title and that string of German names and became John O. Meusebach, citizen of Texas. Then, as more immigrants crowded in, he led a group of his fellow Germans up north a ways from New Braunfels and founded Fredericksburg in 1846. The next year he took his life in his hands and went far out beyond the frontier to make a treaty with the Comanche war chiefs who had been angered by an ill-timed expedition out of Fredericksburg against them. The Indians, in admiration of his bravery and his red beard, called Meusebach "El Sol Colorado" (The Red Sun). The treaty was only moderately successful, but it gave the Comanches three thousand dollars and it gave Fredericksburg time to get established.

The German colonists made a separate world. Speaking their own language, building and planting by European methods, even printing their own German newspapers, they were hard for other Texans to mix with. Not that there were no impractical idealists and dreamers among them. Quite a few of the firstcomers were teachers, musicians, painters, poets—highly educated and unacquainted with practical labor. Among the Texas Germans there were five communities called the "Latin Settlements" because their inhabitants were said to conduct everyday affairs in Latin—Bettina, Sisterdale, and Tusculum in the Hill Country were of that number. But where other colonization attempts had failed because the artists and professional workers were unable to accept the physical demands of the frontier, the Germans, led by Meusebach, who was an internationally known naturalist, learned to change their work habits and agricultural practices to accommodate their new environment—yet at the same time they preserved their traditions of musical organizations, group singing, painting, and academic skills. (Most of Texas's noted early painters and musicians were, in fact, Germans.)

Among the Germans there was little of the frontier restlessness that afflicted the ever-westering Anglo-Americans. Cut off, literally and linguistically, from much communication with the rest of Texas, they clustered by families, then by communities, in a self-constructed society. Even when farming some distance from town, the German families would usually make it in for church services or *saengerfests* on Sundays. This practice led to the quaint (and now valuable) Sunday houses of Fredericksburg, built by farm families so they would have a place to stay when they made their periodic visits into town.

Almost as soon as the Germans began settling up the Hill Country, a number of Anglo families came in, too. At first there was friction, mainly because the Germans were not slaveholders and didn't try to hide their opposition to the practice. They attempted to avoid the inevitable collision, once the Civil War began, some by fleeing to Mexico and others by simply withdrawing to their isolated homesteads. And not all were so opposed to the Confederacy. Many Germans, especially from Comal, Travis, and Bexar counties, fought for the South. But tragedy was inescapable, given the passions of the day. In August, 1862, when sixty-five German Unionists tried to go from Kendall County to Mexico, they were ambushed by a Confederate force; nineteen of them were killed in the fight, then nine more, who were wounded, were summarily executed. Six Germans who escaped were killed a few weeks later while trying to ford the Rio Grande. (A monument in Comfort commemorates those killed, said to be the only locally raised Union monument in a former Confederate state.)

The war and its bewildering test of loyalties, and the enmities aroused, caused the Germans to draw even closer among themselves. Even latecoming immigrants from Germany complained that the people of New Braunfels and Fredericksburg were clannish. And despite the fact that many of them were third-generation Americans by then, there was a good deal of resentment expressed against "the Dutchmen" in Texas during World War I. By World War II this fear was gone, and one of the most famous of the military leaders of that war, Fleet Admiral Chester A. Nimitz, was born and raised in Fredericksburg of an old, famous family and

attended high school in Kerrville. This old bias served, for a long time, to protect the idiosyncracies of the region and the people who live in it.

Traditional German thrift and making best use of available resources probably account as much for the position the Hill Country Germans occupy in the Texas mind as do German sausage, oompah bands, and beer halls. Of course this matter-of-fact approach to life can get out of hand in the presence of genius, as evidenced in the career of Jacob Brodbeck, a schoolteacher and inventor who, in 1863, contrived a small flying machine (that flew!) which had a rudder, wings, and an airscrew (as the propeller was called) turned by coiled springs. Brodbeck got so enthusiastic over his creation that he quit teaching, moved his wife Maria and their twelve children to Luckenbach, and began traveling over the country trying to raise money to manufacture his contrivance, but with little success, save in Gillespie County. Finally Maria got tired of his aerial experimentation and threw his airplane in the creek—according to legend—thus denying Luckenbach the chance to have become the Texas Kitty Hawk.

The Hill Country, with its higher, drier climate, early gained a reputation for being healthy, and several medical figures—including some immigrant German physicians—opened healing retreats, relying mainly on natural cures and hydropathy. Not only were summers more comfortable, but the year-round environment was considered ideal for halting tuberculosis. Kerrville, through the years, has had from four to six hospitals in operation at any one time. Jimmie Rodgers, the fabled "Singing Brakeman" and "Blue Yodler," moved to Kerrville in 1928 for the "TB cure" (he recorded a song called "The TB Blues") and built a costly mansion which he named the Blue Yodler's Paradise. He remained in Texas until his death in 1933.

The Hill Country is a region of summer camps, most of them located around Kerrville, Ingram, and Hunt. Generations of youngsters have spent summers at such celebrated camps as

Mystic, Longhorn, Waldemar, Arrowhead, Stewart, Chrysalis, and Kickapoo, while several religious denominations have encampments around Hunt. When dude ranches (now more politely termed "guest ranches") were introduced in Texas, it was natural that the Hill Country, especially around Bandera, should be the site of some of the most successful. Today these layouts furnish a setting for everything from society cattle auctions to high-fashion showings. Show barns, where the livestock auctions reach their peak of social impact, are a rapidly growing Hill Country phenomenon, fed by the private jet and Texas chic. Newspapers and magazine writers and television crews are on hand to record the high-priced modern enhancement of an old-timey Hill Country trade day and swap meet.

But if summer is a time for invasion by city dwellers to put their children in camp, and themselves to retreat to their summer places, autumn is the time for an even bigger mass attack on the peace of the countryside. Deer season opens. Deer leases (the renting of land by the day or week for hunting) are now a major commodity of the Hill Country, some landowners being able to make as much in two or three months of hunting as their fathers or grandfathers made in several seasons of growing cotton or raising cattle, sheep, and goats. Freezer plants, to handle the annual kill, dot the landscape on and off the main roads. And such locally produced dainties as deer sausage, venison roast and steaks, and venison barbecue are offered in cafes and at big catered parties. One offshoot of this annual hunters' invasion has been the creation of several private hunting preserves—the YO Ranch is perhaps the best known—that are stocked with exotic game animals from around the globe that can be hunted at rather splendid costs per gun per day, and usually by means of rather splendid facilities. Many big corporations have built retreats for corporate officers and friends in the Hill Country; such hideaways are approached, in the main, by air.

Dallas and Houston, at one point, bade fair to take over Fredericksburg and its unique Sunday House and *fachwerk* architecture. What has happened is that both cities, particularly Dallas, contributed great sums which enabled the city of Fredericksburg to be more or less restored to its nineteenth-century glory, even to the resurrection of the "Coffee Mill" church and the steamboat-inspired Nimitz Hotel. Luckenbach, for over a century a quiet little country store, post office, *bierstube*, and dance hall, became elevated to international fame in the 1970s when country singers began praising it as the ultimate spot for retreating from the cold, hard-running world, whether they'd been to Luckenbach or not. The worst thing about Luckenbach's new fame hasn't been the disruption of its rural quiet—after all, the last of the original line of owners sold it years ago—but that souvenir hunters consistently steal the Luckenbach highway signs and cult followers can't find the place.

But men and cities aside, the heart of the Hill Country still belongs to nature. From time to time it has seen men come seeking gold and silver from its earth and profits from its ambience, but it has yielded more legend than lucre. True, the cities of San Antonio, Austin, Houston, and Dallas have invested a good bit of money in city-flavored Hill Country real-estate developments, but only its edges have become urbanized. What attracted people to the Hill Country is still there and has little to do with the changes made by the societies that entered its domain. You don't need to get on the river, as at Wimberly or Blanco, or stand beside one of those magnificent old uncharted stone structures that dot the hills. You can reach a state of lost bliss (or blissful lostness, if that's acceptable) just by reaching the top of a ridge and looking off down a valley that may or may not have the remains of three or four generations of lives in it. The Hill Country hasn't been contained by Texas as yet, and I feel pretty sure it won't be contained in my lifetime.

A. C. GREENE

May, 1981

THE TEXAS HILL COUNTRY
INTERPRETATIONS BY THIRTEEN ARTISTS

Stone Barn

This painting was inspired by German barns of the Hill Country, which were built in stages and might have grown larger with each generation. First stone was laid, then milled lumber was added. This is a composite of typical barns seen along the backroads of the region.

ANCEL E. NUNN

Waterfall

This scene is actually a composite of Hill Country limestone cliffs along shallow streams, with small waterfalls and cool caves full of maidenhair ferns.

WILLIAM HOEY

Cabin and Maples, Sabinal Canyon

This old cabin in the Sabinal Canyon has as its background the sugar maples which give the canyon its vivid beauty, unique in this region. Standing watch behind are the canyon's rugged hills. I took the liberty of transporting the tumbledown fence from another location in the canyon.

E. M. "Buck" Schiwetz

Rocks, Medina River

I painted this watercolor one sunny afternoon about five miles west of Medina on the Medina River. Swimming in the clear, cool water was a welcome relief after spending some time in the sun painting the rocks in the foreground. I decided to concentrate on the rocks and paint them in some detail in order to learn about them. As I was doing so, a bumblebee buzzed around in my Prussian blue, accounting for some of the interesting textural development in the foreground.

MICHAEL FRARY

Hill Country Fence

Scattered throughout the Hill Country are fences other than barbed-wire ones. There are miles of dry-stacked rock and split rail, the rock rapidly disappearing into masonry construction. This fenceline, with a background of pecan, cypress, oak, and cedar trees, was near Verde Creek, west of Kerrville.

RALPH WHITE

Autumn at the Lake

The view through a redbud tree on the deck of the house at Lake Travis was all that was needed to get me started on this painting. Pastel is now my favorite medium, regardless of subject matter. The wide range of colored chalks spread beside me gives me freedom to express quickly my feelings about the subject while it is fresh on my mind.

EMILY GUTHRIE SMITH

Dry Creek Bed with Armadillo

My esthetic philosophy in painting is concerned with the transformation of visual and emotional experiences from the natural world into a unique and personal statement rather than a display of virtuoso technique capable only for the rendering of a stiff photographic image, accurate and dull.

KELLY FEARING

Alert

I am always thrilled by the early-morning mist that occurs in the Hill Country in the late fall, but I doubt that the deer population can appreciate the beauty while the hunting season is at a fever pitch. I have tried to show the concern of the deer in this painting of a dry creek bed that leads into the main stream of the Guadalupe near Comfort.

IVAN MCDOUGAL

Lake Austin

Testimony of geological history is spectacularly evident where the Colorado River flows through the Balcones Fault. The Tom Miller Dam in west Austin creates Lake Austin, a twenty-mile scenic reservoir and the eastern boundary of the Hill Country.

RALPH WHITE

North Fork, Guadalupe

I did this painting as a demonstration for my watercolor workshop at the Hill Country Arts Foundation at Ingram. The locale of the painting is one of the low-water crossings four miles west of Hunt. The strong mullein plants growing out of the rocks in the sunlight appealed to me in contrast to the dark shapes across the river. One of my students told me that many of these big trees with flared trunks are not cypresses but are a type of sequoia.

MICHAEL FRARY

Old Barn, New Horse, Camp Verde

This is a painting I did on the spot at Camp Verde, between Kerrville and Bandera, which was built in 1855 by the U.S. Army as the site of an experiment in the use of camels in the West. The remains of the camel corral may still be seen on location just to the right of the tractor in the painting. This cypress barn is a fine old pyramidal structure still in use. I put the modern tractor and the young horse in to contrast with the obvious age of the barn.

MICHAEL FRARY

Landscape with White Peacock

Many of my landscapes have been inspired by the flora and fauna of the Hill Country near Austin and elsewhere. I'm a great one for picking up and safekeeping those limestone rocks with holes and crevices, lines and textured surfaces, that litter our landscape. My selections ultimately become the model for a huge rock, as in this painting, and often a mountain.

KELLY FEARING

Rock Pool

This is my collective impression of the many rock pools to be found along watercourses in the Hill Country, be they river or stream. Clear and spring-fed, they have their own particular beauty, and it seemed appropriate that they be interpreted through the medium of watercolor.

JOHN GUERIN

47

Stream

Here, I put together a conglomeration of Hill Country stream, grasses, cacti, limestone rocks, and hills.

WILLIAM HOEY

A Walk in the Hills

A Sunday afternoon family walk in the limestone outcropping of the Balcones Fault on the western borders of Austin offered discovery of an occasional arrowhead, varied fossils, and subject matter for this painting.

RALPH WHITE

Toward Fredericksburg

The ranch land of the Hill Country, with its grass, scrubby trees, and rock outcroppings, has long appealed to me as subject matter for painting.

WILLIAM LESTER

53

Portrait of a River

On the headwaters of the Frio River, just below the Prade Ranch, the old road winds up the bed of the river, sometimes in boulder-strewn canyons under sheer cliffs and sometimes through broad, flat bedrock patches. One gray winter morning, the light struck the river-ribbon, making it shine in a thin strip which contrasted dramatically with the dark hills and gray rocks. One lone sycamore became a subtle focal point to sum up this rather moody portrait of a usually quite happy river.

CLAY McGAUGHY

River Road

One of my favorite automobile drives thirty years ago was the road following the Guadalupe River from New Braunfels to Sattler. This was an intimate and winding route passing rocky bluffs and farmhouses and barns within a few feet of the road.

WILLIAM LESTER

Summer River

Here, undammed, the river is wild and fresh—a place to picnic, a place to wade, or just a spot to relax and listen to the birds.

Emily Guthrie Smith

The Train Doesn't Stop Here Anymore

The railroad station has about vanished from the Hill Country. At one time it was the focal point of activity and livelihood for many. This rendition attempts to reflect a proud monument of that time in the past.

E. Gordon West

61

River Cliff

This is a color sketch, combining brush work and pallette knife. The scene is typical of the flat water areas near the low-water crossings that still are found over many streams of the Hill Country.

WILLIAM HOEY

Blue Springs

It seemed that the dramatic sky painted as a reflection, dotted with colorful autumn leaves, would be a more creative approach for this subject, a very peaceful spot to share with others.

EMILY GUTHRIE SMITH

Pipe Creek

I was turned on by this back-lighted view of a spot along Pipe Creek, with its interesting rock textures and the sycamores silhouetted against the sky, and I couldn't resist the challenge of trying to capture the essence of the scene in watercolor.

IVAN MCDOUGAL

Canyon Wall

The most freely interpreted of my work reproduced here, this pastel of a towering canyon wall flanked by trees suggests the potential of a medium I have long neglected. I was particularly pleased with the almost Giotto-esque character of the wall, which, simply rendered, achieves a certain monumentality.

JOHN GUERIN

69

Circle J Ranch near Wimberly

Jeannette and Leon Jaworski own this vast Hill Country spread near Wimberly. I have visited here twice, sketching, indulging in its scenic beauty—the areas of water, the wealth of native trees and flowers, of animals and birds. The lake at sundown harbored coots, teal, and other wild fowl, while deer and turkeys drank at the edge. A great blue heron stood regally by, surveying his kingdom.

E. M. "BUCK" SCHIWETZ

Circle J Ranch — Wimberley

Wagonwheel

Old wagons still dot the Texas Hill Country landscape, evoking thoughts of a bygone era. They are monuments to the settlement of the land and provide fine subject matter for the artist.

E. GORDON WEST

Dawn Ascension

I could see this hill from my studio porch in Hunt. Watching the morning sun go down the side of the hill was a nice way to start a day.

WOODY GWYN

Road to Lampasas

The elements of earth, sky, man, and a moment in time combined in visual interpretation of a "Hill Country presence" in this painting.

RALPH WHITE

Quiet Pond

This peaceful spot is on a ranch just out of Leakey owned by a friend and former high school classmate of mine, Jack Auld. We have spent many enjoyable weekends here painting, swimming in the cold, invigorating Frio River, and just plain loafing.

IVAN McDOUGAL

LBJ Rock

This rock sits in the North Fork of the Guadalupe at Camp Stewart and is one of my favorite spots in the Hill Country.

WOODY GWYN

River Moss

The jade green moss on blue reflected sky makes an exciting abstract pattern, with a touch of red in the reflection of a figure added for excitement. This scene is at the foot of the dam on the Guadalupe River near Hunt, Texas.

EMILY GUTHRIE SMITH

The Baldwin House near Ingram

The Baldwin house on the South Fork of the Guadalupe near Ingram remains one of the early farmhouses in Kerr County. It has long been one of my favorite subjects with its excellent design and its fine use of native wood and rock. Even the outbuildings are well proportioned. Any of them contains trunks and chests of lace, embroidery, and other handwork which have remained unmolested through the years.

E. M. "BUCK" SCHIWETZ

The Baldwin House near Ingham

Bull Creek

Just north and west of Austin, and lying directly in the path of numerous suburban developments, Bull Creek is represented here as it was just a few years ago. Then a beautiful, clear stream that thinned in the summer but never ran dry, it flowed between high bluffs and grassy meadows, alternately narrowing and widening to create miniature falls and rapids or wide, still pools.

JOHN GUERIN

Summer Heat

This painting displays the heat of a summer day at the edge of the Hill Country. Here, in contrast with the cool rivers and lakes, the brilliance of the shimmering heat on the tin roofs and in the blank, pink gray sky dazzles the eye. Again, the versatility of the pastel medium is shown.

EMILY GUTHRIE SMITH

Stopping Place

Although this is not a specific locale, it is about the country around Mason. Certain stretches of Beaver Creek and the James River, which run into the Llano, burble around granite outcroppings and red "artistic" sandbars, giving the whole country a sort of "rusty" look. It's a look of the Old West still. I expect these old boys have ridden a long way over the high country, and, as the sun goes down, are happy to have happened on their private oasis. I'd like to camp with them tonight, under the stars, on the James.

CLAY McGAUGHY

Sun through Clouds, Lake Travis

My wife and I had just dropped anchor in this cove at Point Venture near Lakeway after sailing up Lake Travis from the Austin Yacht Club. The sun coming through the storm clouds to the west was impressive, so I tried to express the mood of impending violence from the back of the boat. After I did this painting the storm hit, but my three anchors held. I have experienced storms on Lake Travis in which the wind comes suddenly, like a wall of water, accelerating from zero to seventy miles per hour in five seconds or less.

MICHAEL FRARY

Luckenbach Store

Luckenbach is one of those absolutely unique places, quite different from any other place I had ever been. The store—really three stores in one—was a meeting place for farmers who sat in the rear in the *Bierstube* and swapped stories, a general store for the ladies who did their shopping there, and the administrative connection with the outside world through the post office. Benno Engel single-handedly ran all three parts of the store, simultaneously, and wondered what would happen to his store if he should ever leave.

ANCEL E. NUNN

The Killdeer

This painting was initially begun as a study of rock textures and water reflections which I chanced upon during one of our weekend paintouts, but I couldn't resist including one of my favorite Hill Country residents, the killdeer, usually called "killdee" in these parts. You'll find him around any of the streams that crisscross the area.

IVAN McDOUGAL

97

River Bluff

The geological structure of the earth has given me constant stimulus for much of the painting I have done. *River Bluff* is based on the rugged country along the Pedernales a few miles before this river flows into the Colorado.

WILLIAM LESTER

Wildflowers

Parts of the Hill Country are flat fields full of beautiful wild-flowers in spring. Trees and hills lie far in the distance, and a big sky hangs above.

WILLIAM HOEY

Battle Canyon

Stepping gradually upward from the Pedernales River, Battle Canyon records the turbulence that occasionally descends this dry creek bed. Its limestone floor, etched and sculpted by water action, is lined with dense stands of cedar and oak—seemingly unchanged since a vanished people fought their last battle here.

JOHN GUERIN

The Field That Was Overlooked

In essence, this painting is a portrait of my wife Jane overlooking a field in the Hill Country. She is in a meditative mood brought about by a nostalgic and somber landscape.

E. Gordon West

German Farm House

I had serious thoughts about living in the Luckenbach area. With the help of local people, we looked at a number of limestone houses built long before the turn of the century. I then realized this country was steeped in tradition and customs unique only to itself.

ANCEL E. NUNN

Coon Fishing

This little painting was commissioned some years ago by my friend, that grand lady, now deceased, Anne Burnette Windfohr Tandy as a gift for her friend Frank Wardlaw.

KELLY FEARING

Lake in the Hills

I was first impressed with the sequence of lakes upstream on the Colorado River from Austin during World War II, when I was an air force pilot. The contrasts of rhythmic hills, twisted cedar stumps, blue waters, and the massive Mansfield Dam provided stimulus for this painting in the mid-1950's. Now, twenty-five years later, I am nearing completion of a studio-gallery-home only a short distance from this site.

RALPH WHITE

Clean Carpet

In 1973 it snowed twice in and north of San Antonio. Since sticking snows are rather rare this far south, I hustled around those days with my camera and recorded. The weather watcher me has always enjoyed snow, and I still react to it like a kid. The artist me finds it a great tool to simplify with. What would be a rather complicated subject is whittled down to a simple, bold design without a lot of complicated and superfluous detail. It allows a simple statement. Perhaps you can feel the softness and hear the silence. I did that day.

CLAY McGAUGHY

Wet Spring

The simple elegance of this hillside, after a shower, seemed very special. I wanted to express the feeling of early spring, with the first wildflowers (bluebonnets and daisies) following the draw right down to my feet.

EMILY GUTHRIE SMITH

Night Silver

During the day the Guadalupe is a dark vein in the land-scape. It varies from blue to green to brown. But on moonlit nights the tones reverse themselves; the land becomes dark and the river, in places, a glowing silver.

WOODY GWYN

About the Artists

Kelly Fearing received the M.F.A. from Columbia University. His work has been exhibited in national and international exhibitions and is in the collections of the Dallas Museum of Art; the Museum of Fine Arts, Houston; the Milwaukee Art Center; the Institute of Contemporary Art, Boston; the Fort Worth Art Center; and numerous private collections. He is professor of art at the University of Texas at Austin.

Michael Frary received the B.Arch. and the M.F.A. in painting from the University of Southern California. He is author of *Impressions of the Big Thicket* and *Impressions of the Texas Panhandle* and a contributor to *The Texas Gulf Coast*. His highly awarded work has received special recognition by the National Gallery of Art. He is professor of art at the University of Texas at Austin.

John Guerin studied at the American Academy of Art, Chicago; Art Students League, New York; Colorado Springs Fine Arts Center; and Escuela de Bellas Artes, Mexico. His works are held in many permanent collections and have been exhibited at the Metropolitan Museum of Art, the Corcoran Gallery of Art, and the Whitney Museum of Fine Arts, among others. At present he is professor of art at the University of Texas at Austin.

Woody Gwyn, a native Texan, studied at the Pennsylvania Academy of Fine Art. A resident of the Hill Country until the mid-1970's, he now lives in New Mexico. His work is represented by the Heydt-Bair Gallery in Santa Fe and the Allen Stone Gallery in New York.

William Hoey received the M.F.A. from the University of Texas at Austin. Exhibitions of his work have appeared in major museums in Houston, Dallas, and Santa Fe. He has received purchase awards from the Texas Fine Arts Association and the Texas Watercolor Society, among others, and he teaches at the University of Texas at Austin, having served as dean of the Houston Museum of Fine Arts school.

William Lester, born in Graham, studied and worked in Dallas until moving to Austin. One-man exhibitions of his work have appeared in New York, Mexico City, Guadalajara, and major cities in Texas. His work is represented in several Texas museums as well as the Metropolitan Museum of Art, the American Academy of Arts and Letters, and the Pennsylvania Academy of Fine Arts. He is professor emeritus of art at the University of Texas at Austin.

Ivan McDougal, born in Lometa, studied art at Trinity University and at the American Academy of Art in Chicago. He has exhibited in many major regional and national shows and has received numerous awards. In 1978 he was Artist of the Year of the San Antonio Art League. He is represented in the permanent collection of the McNay Art Museum, San Antonio, and teaches watercolor at the San Antonio Art Institute.

Clay McGaughy is a San Antonio artist who received his art degree from the University of Texas. His work is shown in galleries throughout the nation, and limited-edition prints of eighteen of his paintings have been published. He is a member of several art societies and teaches a course in watercolor at the Hill Country Arts Foundation. He has been featured in *Southwest Art* and has done covers and illustrations for other magazines.

Ancel E. Nunn is from Seymour, Texas. His work has been exhibited in many Texas museums. He has received a number of awards, including the Texas Arts Alliance award and the Chicago '76 Certificate of Excellence. He was guest instructor at the University of Texas at Tyler in 1979–1980, and his studio is in Palestine, Texas.

E. M. "Buck" Schiwetz, born in Cuero, received the B.S. degree in architecture from Texas A&M University. He worked briefly in architecture, later in advertising, and for more than fifty years has painted Texas scenes and structures. His work is represented in major museums and appears in five books and two print portfolios. He was Texas state artist in 1977–1978. He lives in Westhoff.

Emily Guthrie Smith studied at Texas Woman's University, the University of Oklahoma, and the Art Students League, New York. She is winner of many awards, and her works are included in six Texas museums and the Smithsonian Institution. She has taught for fifteen years at the Fort Worth Museum of Fine Arts, in the Special Courses Series at Texas Christian University, and in many workshops in Texas and New Mexico.

E. Gordon West received his B.S. degree from the University of Louisville and did advance study at the Chicago Art Institute. His work has been accepted in numerous competitive exhibitions and has won many awards. He is represented by Glasser's Art Gallery, Odyssey Galleries, and the Sol del Rio Gallery, all in San Antonio.

Ralph White is professor in the Department of Art of the University of Texas at Austin. He has exhibited in more than one hundred group and one-man exhibitions in the Southwest as well as nationally and internationally, and his work is represented in major museums and collections.